Eric Carle

The Tiny Seed

Seed

SCHOLASTIC INC.
New York Toronto London Auckland Sydney

It is Autumn.

A strong wind is blowing. It blows flower seeds high in the air and carries them far across the land. One of the seeds is tiny, smaller than any of the others. Will it be able to keep up with the others? And where are they all going?

One of the seeds flies higher than the others. Up, up it goes! It flies too high and the sun's hot rays burn it up. But the tiny seed sails on with the others.

Another seed lands on a tall and icy mountain.
The ice never melts, and the seed cannot grow.
The rest of the seeds fly on. But the tiny seed
does not go as fast as the others.

Now they fly over the ocean. One seed falls into the water and drowns. The others sail on with the wind. But the tiny seed does not go as high as the others.

One seed drifts down onto the desert. It is hot and dry, and the seed cannot grow. Now the tiny seed is flying very low, but the wind pushes it on with the others.

Finally the wind stops and the seeds fall gently down on the ground. A bird comes by and eats one seed. The tiny seed is not eaten. It is so small that the bird does not see it.

Now it is Winter.
After their long trip the seeds settle down. They look just as if they are going to sleep in the earth. Snow falls and covers them like a soft white blanket. A hungry mouse that also lives in the ground eats a seed for his lunch. But the tiny seed lies very still and the mouse does not see it.

Now it is Spring.
After a few months the snow has melted. It is really spring!
Birds fly by. The sun shines. Rain falls. The seeds grow so
round and full they start to burst open a little.
Now they are not seeds any more. They are plants. First
they send roots down into the earth. Then their little stems
and leaves begin to grow up toward the sun and air.
There is another plant that grows much faster than the
new little plants. It is a big fat weed. And it takes all the
sunlight and the rain away from one of the small new
plants. And that little plant dies.

The tiny seed hasn't begun to grow yet. It will be too late!
Hurry! But finally it too starts to grow into a plant.

The warm weather also brings the children out to play.
They too have been waiting for the sun and spring time.
One child doesn't see the plants as he runs along and —
Oh! He breaks one! Now it cannot grow any more.

The tiny plant that grew from the tiny seed is growing fast,
but its neighbor grows even faster. Before the tiny plant
has three leaves the other plant has seven! And look! A bud!
And now even a flower!

But what is happening? First there are footsteps. Then a shadow looms over them. Then a hand reaches down and breaks off the flower.

A boy has picked the flower to give to a friend.

It is Summer.
Now the tiny plant from the tiny seed is all alone.
It grows on and on. It doesn't stop. The sun shines
on it and the rain waters it. It has many leaves.
It grows taller and taller. It is taller than the people.
It is taller than the trees. It is taller than the houses.
And now a flower grows on it. People come from
far and near to look at this flower. It is the tallest
flower they have ever seen. It is a giant flower.

All summer long the birds and bees and butterflies come visiting. They have never seen such a big and beautiful flower.

Now it is Autumn again.
The days grow shorter. The nights grow cooler. And
the wind carries yellow and red leaves past the flower.
Some petals drop from the giant flower and they sail
along with the bright leaves over the land and down
to the ground.

The wind blows harder. The flower has lost almost all of its petals. It sways and bends away from the wind. But the wind grows stronger and shakes the flower. Once more the wind shakes the flower, and this time the flower's seed pod opens. Out come many tiny seeds that quickly sail far away on the wind.

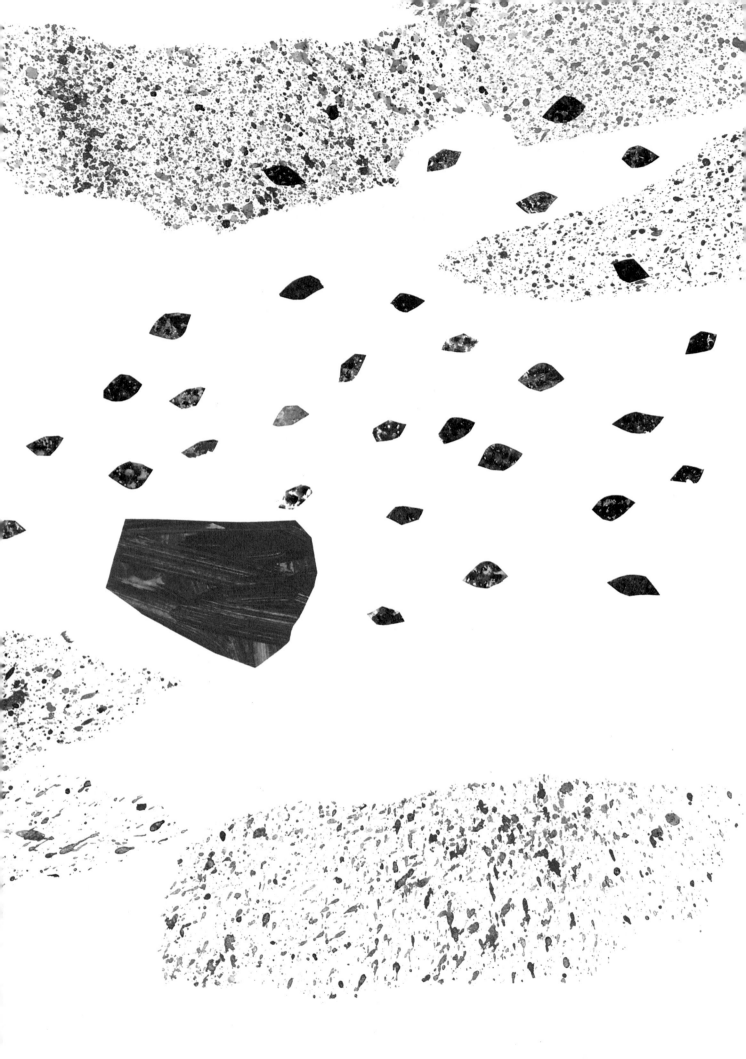

ISBN 0-590-42566-8

60 59 58 57 56   10 11 12 / 0
Printed in the U.S.A.   08
First Scholastic printing, April 1989